ANGELS, ANGELS, ANGELS

Landrum P. Leavell

Nashville, Tennessee

4222-22
ISBN: 0-8054-2222-6

Library of Congress Catalog Card Number: 73-75627

Printed in the United States of America

To four of God's greatest and best
gifts to me: Lan, Ann, Roland, and David

CONTENTS

PREFACE

These chapters are basically sermons which were first preached to congregations where I have been privileged to serve. For the most part they have been used periodically in morning services of revivals where I have preached, for it seems that they have spoken to common, everyday human experience.

There is no way to give credit to all those to whom I am indebted for helpful insights and encouragement in the preparation and delivery of these sermons. I have continued to read since graduation from the seminary, and everything I have read has contributed to what I am and what I stand for.

Projects such as this little volume would be impossible without the understanding and support of the fellowship of believers where I am pastor. My often stated conviction is that the First Baptist Church, Wichita Falls, Texas, is the "finest, friendliest church on the face of the earth." These beloved friends possess a spiritual maturity and depth of love that makes my calling the highest and best of all.

My family is one of my greatest sources of inspiration. My wife, Jo Ann, and my four children, Lan, Ann, Roland and David make life worth living and are wonderfully understanding when they have an "absentee" daddy. My home is my castle, and I am never really happy when separated from it and from those who make it my "little heaven on earth."

The staff of First Baptist Church is professional in the noblest sense of the word, and have relieved me of innumerable details to enable me to complete projects like this. I am indebted to the pastor's secretary, Mrs. Otis Grafa, for her patience, understanding, and willingness to complete the typing of this manuscript. These staff members are not only my closest associates, but are among my closest friends.

My only purpose in publishing this material is the hope that the wider distribution of it might mean the salvation of lost persons and strengthening of God's people.

1

THE PRESENCE OF ANGELS

1 Peter 3:22

The study of angelology is one of the most intriguing a Christian may pursue. It is inseparably connected with the supernatural. The statements made in the Bible regarding angels cannot be explained in naturalistic terms. For those who reject a belief in the supernatural, this volume will be utterly without value. On the other hand, if you believe that God is who he said he is, that he possesses the power attributed to him, if you are a believer in the supernatural, the things that will be said will be on your wave length and will have meaning for you.

In view of the rising tide of demonism, spiritism, astrology, and fortune-telling, a study of angels takes on greater importance. There are probably some people who believe in angels who've been led off on a tangent, away from the Bible and the clear truths of God. And so I pray we'll be able to get our feet on the solid rock and determine what God's Word says and how it fits us in this day and age.

Very little attention is given to this subject today. As I have said before, I do not recall ever in my lifetime having heard a sermon on angels. I have read some since I began this study, but I don't recall ever having heard one coming from a pulpit or a preacher under whose ministry I sat.

One reason this entire subject has been disregarded is that during the Middle Ages angelology fell into disrepute. The scholastics of that day, the scholars, reduced the study of angelology to a debate over how many angels could dance on the head of a pin. Because of the ridiculousness of this, many people pushed the entire matter out of their minds and ceased to give consideration to it.

Also during the Middle Ages there was an attempt on the part of scholars to build a case for a physical function for angels. You'll recall the story in Genesis in which Lot, living in the area of Sodom and Gomorrah, was approached by angels. It was said that the angels went into Lot's house and he provided food for them. On the basis of that text some scholars went to great lengths to try to prove biblically that they had a physical function, that their bodies operated in the same way as yours and mine, that they had hunger and all of the other necessities of our bodies.

Unbelief is another reason for our neglect of this study, for people today associate angels in the same category with Santa Claus, the Easter bunny, fairies, and gremlins. When you talk about angels, many take a mental jump and go off in that direction. Honestly, if I were to ask you to reveal your deepest, most sincere thoughts at this point, many of you would have to admit you're not sure what you believe about angels. Because of this we've disregarded the study and made little effort to find what God's Word teaches us on the subject.

To many the entire matter seems irrelevant, and that's why there has been very little emphasis on it in our preaching ministry or personal Bible study. In other words there are those who say, "So what? What if there are angels? What difference will this make to me? If I happen to believe in angels, is it going to make a difference in the way I keep my house, drive my car, work at my business, or serve Christ in the church?" Because of a feeling of irrelevance many people have turned away from the study of angels. I believe that this is a tremendously important subject. At the outset I want us to see some

REASONS

for its importance. I want us to establish these first of all. Then we'll come to a realization and finally we'll look at our reaction to what we know on the basis of what we've said and learned tonight.

The basic reason for believing in angels is the Bible teaches it! If you believe the Bible, you have to accept this part. There are 108 places in the Old Testament where angels are mentioned and 165 places in the New Testament. They are seen all through sacred history from the earliest records of the history of man, found in the book of Genesis, all the way through the New Testament era and the writings of the book of the Revelation.

There's no point in sacred history where there was not a strong, firm conviction concerning angels. It is true that the emphasis on angels has fluctuated across the centuries. But from the time God placed an angel at the entrance of the garden to keep Adam and Eve from returning, biblical history has demonstrated a belief in angels. Their activities in heaven and on earth in the past are recorded in both Testaments, and interestingly enough, their future manifestation is prophetically revealed. Angels are going to have a great deal to do with the end of the world, the second coming of Christ, and the judgment. They're going to be the reapers in that day. Jesus said so. They will separate the sheep and goats, the tares and the wheat, left and right. The New Testament gives great emphasis to the ministry of angels.

You'll recall in the New Testament that a religious group called the Sadducees rejected the reality or presence of angels (see Acts 23:8). The Sadducees of Jesus' day find their counterpart in the theological liberals of our day in that they rejected the doctrine of angelology. The Sadducees were probably the first theological liberals, but their tribe has continued to this hour. There are many, many people who claim to be under the banner of the Cross who nevertheless deny the clear teachings of the Word of God on this vital subject. That's the first reason for belief in angels: the Bible teaches it.

Secondly, Jesus believed in them and taught us concerning their ministry. This again is a very telling reason. It has great weight in the life of any born again believer, a follower of Jesus Christ, who believes the Word of God. Jesus spoke any number of times of angels and always associated them with his own glory. If we deny the existence of angels, we charge the Lord Jesus Christ with falsehood. We accuse him of being a liar. Either there are angels or there are not. Jesus believed there were. If there are no angels, Jesus was deceived. Such a charge against Jesus implies his fallibility and rejects his diety. If Jesus told a lie, he was not sinlessly perfect, he was not God in human flesh with all knowledge, but he was a man just like you or me. So if we reject a belief in angels, in that same breath we have rejected Jesus

Christ the Son of God.

Another very important reason for this study and our belief in angels is because of their earthly ministry. Are you familiar with Hebrews 1:14? If not, you ought to underscore that verse, for pointedly, clearly, we're told that angels have an earthly ministry. It's clearly taught that their assistance is given to the individual believer who performs a divine service for Christ and the kingdom.

If these reasons are valid, why is it that we don't talk more about angels? Why is it that we don't study more of them? I think perhaps it's due to our affluence. This has adversely affected our study of the subject. This has kept many of us from making a detailed study of the Word of God in general. We don't think we need it. We don't think we have any need that we cannot supply ourselves. The present prosperity of the church leads us to indifference toward the guardianship of angels. Who needs angels? We've got money, we think. Like the church in Laodicea, far too many of us as individual Christians have the attitude attributed to them. They said, "I am rich and increased with goods and in need of nothing." You'll recall it was against that church Jesus Christ gave one of the bitterest denunciations recorded in all of literature, sacred or secular. They thought they had it made!

The fires of martyrdom burned out centuries ago. If you and I were gripped by the lurking fear that when we left our churches we would be apprehended by the police or gestapo, that we would be incarcerated in some prison or jail, and that we would possibly be called upon to give our lives for the very privilege of being in a worship service, we would believe in guardian angels! We would believe in the providence of God. We would depend upon him far more than we presently do.

Instruments of torture are not used in our day and generation. We've become civilized along with our affluence. Christians are no longer persecuted and this is one of the reasons we find such spiritual indifference in our land and such a great misunderstanding regarding this all important prayer amendment being discussed by our Congress. Why are we indifferent to it? It's because Baptists, who always stood against the establishment of religion, in other times stood to lose a great deal. Today we have Baptist representatives in Austin, we have them in the Court House in Wichita Falls, we have them in Washington, so we'll run this show. We'll make other people do it our way. But when Baptists came to the United States we were such a woeful minority that we stood, and our parents, grandparents, and great grandparents even gave their lives to assure that no government would ever dictate anything religious to anybody in this free land. If they pass a prayer amendment, government will be dictating religion, and the same government that can dictate religion can dictate against religion and forbid worship.

The fires of martyrdom no longer burn. We don't have the need of dependence on angels, for we think we have everything. We're in a majority. Christians in America are a large part of the population. There are more of us than any other religious group; so we don't fear things that could be real dangers.

We don't depend on angels, we don't look to the ministry of God through these celestial beings in our behalf. Probably our affluence is the reason for it. Enemies of the cross today live in peaceful coexistence with the followers of the Lamb. So these are some of the reasons for a study of this doctrine. But let's move now to a

REALIZATION

that needs to come to all of us. It's a realization that involves a distinction. The name angel both in Hebrew and Greek means messenger. The Greek word *angelos* designates an office rather than designating a person.

In the Hebrew the word "angel" is the same as the name of the last book of the Old Testament, Malachi. That's the Hebrew word for angel. Malachi means, my angel, or my messenger. So Malachi was God's messenger. *Agelos* is a messenger. This is an office; it's a function, not so much a person.

We must possess a realization of the difference between the ministry of the Holy Spirit and the ministry of angels. Some people ask, "What's the difference? It's all the same." No, it isn't. The Holy Spirit has been given the peculiar responsibility of interpreting and revealing Jesus Christ and imparting the truth of God. The Holy Spirit reveals Jesus to you and me. He's the One who makes us know we're lost. He's the One who makes us know that only Jesus can save, that we can't save ourselves, that this is something he does. The Holy Spirit brings this conviction. He's the divine Interpreter, providing both revelation and information in spiritual matters. The Holy Spirit functions in spiritual matters.

Angels, however, appear to have been given the administration of physical things. Let me give you a few instances. In the Old Testament, when Hagar was fainting in the wilderness, an angel appeared as the Lord's captain and provided a sword. In the New Testament, when the apostle Peter was in prison it was an angel that drew back the iron bolts from the prison gate and led him out of prison to safety. Again in the Old Testament it was an angel who appeared to Gideon making a sign out of the kid, the cakes, and the broth, which he had prepared, but it was the Spirit of God that followed up in Gideon's case, who qualified Gideon for his work.

Now we're going to talk much more at length about the ministry of angels to Jesus Christ, but keep in mind that our Lord was led by the Spirit, taught by the Spirit, filled with the Spirit, but he was fed physically by angels, and strengthened by angels. Jesus was led up into the wilderness by the Spirit to be tempted. But after the temptations, when the Devil left the scene of the battle for a season, it was the angels who came and ministered to his physical needs (Matt. 4:1, 11). This is what the New Testament teaches of the ministry of angels. It's a physical ministry. Their watchcare has brought us through those narrow escapes, those times when we looked death in the face and miraculously were spared. That physical ministry, that watchcare, that protection is the ministry of angels according to the teachings of the Word.

Another interesting distinction that needs to be made, as part of our realization of the presence of angels, involves the difference between the law and the gospel. The law, according to Acts 7:53, Galatians 3:19, and Hebrews 2:2, was spoken by angels. It was engraved on material or physical tablets of stone. Here again, the ministry is material or physical. But the gospel which is ministered by the Holy

Spirit and revealed to the heart of man, exalting Jesus Christ through his ministry, is not written on physical tablets of stone like the Ten Commandments. The gospel is written on the spiritual tables of the heart. Second Corinthians 3:3 points out this truth. The ministry of the Holy Spirit is a spiritual ministry as the Interpreter who reveals Jesus. The ministry of angels is a ministry to the physical and material needs of humanity. If these are truths found in the Word of God, what is our

REACTION

The first possibility is that we may scoff, shrug our shoulders, laugh and say, "So what?" Many who claim to believe the Bible smile with condescension upon any allusion to angels. If you really believe that the Bible is God's revelation to man, that it is God's Holy Word, then this is a part of that revelation. If we accept the scoffers' stance, we identify ourselves with the Sadducees who state there is no resurrection, neither angels nor spirit. If we identify ourselves with the Sadducees of old, we have taken our stand along with the liberal theologians who mock and scorn the basic truths of the Christian faith.

There is a second possibility. We may scoff, or we may study. With 273 references to angels found in the Bible, any serious student of the Word of God must confront this subject and construct a doctrine of angelology. I think that the one center pole in our study must be the word that we have chosen as our text, 1 Peter 3:22. It's there we read that our Lord has authority over angels and everything else. This study basically involves a study of the Lordship of Jesus Christ, who has dominion over principalities, over powers, over things past, over things present and things yet to come. He exercises total Lordship over the ministry of angels in your life and mine. So as we continue this study in the weeks to come, let's do so with the prayer that Jesus Christ shall be exhalted and that he shall be the Lord of our hearts.

2

THE PRODUCTION OF ANGELS

Job 38:4-7

The Bible is unapologetically supernatural. From Genesis all the way through to the Revelation we see a record of how God has intervened in human affairs. Each intervention of God is supernatural. By that I mean it cannot be explained by natural causes. These are things in the biblical record which God accomplished by injecting himself into the affairs of men. I'm convinced that the only cure for the materialism of our day is to discover and believe what the Scriptures reveal regarding the spirit world. There's just one thin veil between our natural world and the spirit world. That thin veil is the experience we call death.

The spirit world began with time and was created by the power of God. It seems clear, according to the biblical record, that angels came into existence prior to the creation of the material world and, without any shadow of doubt, angels were created prior to man. The sequence seems to be in the Word of God: first, the creation of the purely spiritual, including angels and all the spirit world; and then the material universe, followed by the creation of man, who is partly material and partly spiritual. I believe that sequence can be substantiated in the teachings of the Book. Let me say in the first place, as my beginning point, that the production of angels was from

DIETY

That is, it was of God. In Psalm 148 verses 1–5, we find these words: "Praise ye him, all his angels . . . for he [that is, God] commanded, and they were created." That's a significant truth, and one that we will do well to remember. In Colossians 1:16 we read: "For by him [that is, Jesus Christ the eternal Logos] were all things created, that are in heaven, and that are in earth, visible and invisible, whether they be thrones, or dominions, or principalities, or powers: all things were created by him, and for him." So the existence of angels simply says that the creative power of Jesus Christ was released in their production. They were produced by diety.

It seems that there was a false teaching among Christians that exalted angels. This led to a veneration, or even a worship, of angels. Perhaps that is roughly comparable to what we see today in some denominations involving the veneration of saints. This means that there are certain so-called "patron saints" to whom people look for protective care or other blessings, and by looking to them they have taken their eyes off Jesus Christ. In Colossians 1:16 the apostle Paul could well be striking at such a heresy in regard to angels. His readers believed so strongly in the presence of angels that they began to worship them. Paul pointed out that Jesus Christ, who is the Creator of this earth and all that's in it, also created angels, and he alone is worthy of our worship. I'm saying then, in case you're not yet with me, we do not worship angels! We do not pray to angels! They are created beings, created by the hand of almighty

God through Jesus Christ, and they are here in subjection to him.

These created beings are wholly subject to Jesus Christ. In Job 38:4–7 we read (God is speaking): "Where wast thou when I laid the foundations of the earth . . . when the morning stars sang together [God is referring to a time prior to the creation of man] . . . and all the sons of God shouted for joy?" Aiso, in Job 1:6, we read: "Now that was a day when the sons of God came to present themselves before the Lord, and Satan came also among them." This same truth is found in Job 2:1 These sons of God were angels. They were living witnesses to the creation. They saw what God did in his marvelous, infinite, creative power, not simply in creating this little infinitesimal speck we call the earth, but in creating all the heavenlies—all the solar systems, all the innumerable galaxies of space. Angels were living witnesses to the creation. They were the "morning stars" of that time when God brought into existence something from nothing. Now, these verses point out that angels are created beings. They come from the power of diety. Let's look at their

DESIGNATIONS

There are only two kinds of angels. There are holy angels and fallen angels. We could simply call them good and bad angels. They are aligned with the power of God and the power of the devil.

These living beings are of the highest position imaginable. They are higher in their existence than man. Our text, Psalm 8:5, pointed out that God has made man a little lower than the angels. (The RSV translates the passage "little less than God," but the Hebrew is unclear, so I have adopted the traditional translation, which also agrees with Hebrews 2:6–7.) That means that they are superior to you and me in many of the characteristics they possess. We will go into a little more elaborate discussion of this in a subsequent chapter. I'll point out that there are some ways in which angels are superior to us, but there are also some ways in which we are superior to angels. No angel can witness to the redemptive grace of God! No angel knows what it's like to be saved, for the holy angels have never been lost. They've had no need for salvation, therefore they have not had the privilege that comes to you and me to witness to the saving power of the Lord Jesus Christ.

These celestial, spiritual beings are of the greatest consequence in our universe. The designation of good angels (or holy angels), and fallen angels, (or bad angels), points up the truth that they are free moral beings and have their destiny within the power of their own choice. Like you and me, they have the ability to choose right or wrong. The holy angels have chosen right. The fallen angels have chosen evil. This does not imply that they are independent, any more than we are. This does not say that they are self-originating, self-sustaining, or equal to God. They are not. But they do possess the power of choice, obviously, for Lucifer did and he chose evil.

The number of angels is unknown. The Bible refers to them in many places as hosts. Just as we cannot number the stars or the galaxies of space, neither can we number angels. The number, however, has not been increased or decreased since the beginning. Except for apostasy or desertion, the family of holy angels has remained the same in number since they were called into being by the power of the Father God. In Daniel 7:10 they are referred to as "thousands of thousands." In Revelation 5:11 we get another indication of their number. In the ministry of Jesus we read that he, by the power of God, could have called forth legions of angels to come to his rescue, had he so desired. These angelic hosts are the good angels who've remained faithful after the fall of Lucifer and the rebellious spirits.

The Bible states that Lucifer and the fallen angels sinned and kept not their first state. The Bible points out that the sin of Lucifer was the sin of pride. I've got a whole chapter on this fallen angel. I call him the "perverted" angel.

The sin of pride was that which caused his downfall. My friend, if it would cause the downfall of one who had the majesty and awesomeness of Lucifer in the heavenlies, it most assuredly can cause your downfall and mine. If we wear our feelings on our sleeves, if our lives are marked by pride and vainglory, we're heading for a fall just as surely as Lucifer fell. In 2 Peter 2:4 and in Jude 6 we find that these fallen angels chose evil and kept not their first state.

In his teachings, Jesus pointed out that angels neither marry nor do they die (Luke 20:36). Keep in mind that marriage implies procreation. Procreation meets the necessity of death. The only reason we're here is because of the procreation of our parents, our grandparents, etc. If they had not reproduced themselves, the human race would have been eliminated. This is not true with angels. They have no need for procreation because they do not die. The ranks of angels have neither been increased by procreation, nor have they been decreased by death since God brought them into being in response to his own divine fiat. Their number remains the same. The only division is between good (holy) angels and bad (fallen) angels.

Many people believe that when they die they will become angels. That's not so. You're not going to become an angel when you die, nor is an angel going to become a human being in eternity. When Jesus said that we in the resurrection state will be "equal" to angels, he didn't mean that we were to be identical to them. He rather was pointing out that we, on an equal with angels, would neither marry nor die in eternity. This doesn't mean we're going to become angels. It means we'll take on those characteristics of angels, because in heaven there'll be no marriage and no deaths. Now in the angelic authority I believe we do well to note that there are

DIVISIONS

In Jude 6 reference is made to the angels who "left their own habitation." That clearly establishes the truth that they had an estate given them. God didn't create them without giving them an abode. He gave them an estate. We need not limit our understanding of the abode of angels to this earth. This terrestrial ball which we populate is not the only place angels can reside.

Modern astronomy presents evidence of the vastness of the material creation. Our closest neighbor is the moon. The moon is 240,000 miles removed from the earth. That's almost a quarter of a million miles. It staggers our imagination. When a spaceship is put into space, achieves orbit, and then goes out on its tangent toward the moon, it travels at up to 18,000 miles per hour. What a fantastic speed! But still it takes days to reach the moon. Recently we learned of the progress of Mariner 9. Mariner 9, forgotten by the masses of people of the world, has been on its journey into space for weeks and weeks and weeks on end. Today Mariner 9 is orbiting the red planet, Mars. Mariner 9 is 78 million miles from earth. I don't understand that. I have no comprehension of that vastness in space. Seventy-eight million miles from earth. Can you imagine how many heavenly bodies there are like Mars in the millions and millions and millions of miles that go beyond Mars? And, can you imagine, if there's another Mars 78 million miles from this Mars around which Mariner 9 is now orbiting, another Mars 78 million beyond that, and another 78 million miles beyond that, and on and on and on. The possibility staggers the imagination of man.

God gave angels their own habitation. Where is it? It could be anywhere in space. It could be anywhere in the heavenlies. Solar systems greater than our own are known to exist. Our solar system is conjectured to be one of the innumerable solar systems. Some of these are 30 to 60 billion miles from earth. I can't understand this. I can't grasp infinity. It's beyond my comprehension. In this vast universe, our solar system, our sun represents a single point, a lone dwelling among multiplied millions of possible habitations.

The question always comes, "Is our solar system the greatest in space or the least? Is our planet the only inhabited planet in all of the infinitude of God's creative power? Is this the only globe on which life exists?" Science ventures guesses, but God's Word speaks with authority. Angels dwell in the heavenly spheres and they are there in numbers beyond human computation.

Though there are only two designations, namely holy angels and fallen angels, there are nevertheless ranks and organizations among the holy angels. The angelic hierarchy includes the following divisions: the seraphim, the cherubim, thrones, dominions, mights, powers, principalities, and even an archangel. Now the prefix "arch" implies authority. An archbishop in the Roman Catholic Church is a ruling bishop. An archangel is the ruling angel.

You know, one of the interesting debates I've found in this study of angelology is the difference on the part of many who have studied this subject concerning the number of archangels. Some say there are three, but the Bible only tells us of one. Some say that Michael, Lucifer, and Gabriel all are archangels. But the Bible only refers to one as an archangel, and we're going to study him in greater detail. The fact that there is an archangel signifies rank, divisions, organizations, and authorities. Thrones are greater than lordships; principalities appear to be higher than authority.

Implications of authority accompany each of these divisions. Thrones imply that there are those who sit upon them. Dominions allude to those who rule. Principalities have reference to those who govern. Powers point to those who exercise supremacy. Authorities include those who are invested with imperial responsibility. I believe that it is of greatest comfort to Christians to know that not only on this planet but also all the heavenly bodies of the universe are included in God's protective presence and care day by day.

Space explorations by man didn't take God by surprise. Some of us may have wondered what God thought about all that was going on.

I had a lady in our city call me one night. She was a regular caller for a long time, and then she found that I didn't agree with her and she ceased to call, for which I'm grateful. Her calls always came after 11:30 at night. She was one of those who stays up all night and sleeps all day, and she thought everyone else did. After she awakened me, and my whole family any number of different nights, I tired of our conversations. But this woman stated flatly that there was no such thing as a space probe, that men had not set foot on the moon and this was all "Communist propaganda." I thought that was an interesting theory, and I told her she had a right to believe what she would, but that I just didn't happen to agree. I believe it is true, and told her that I had met an astronaut who had been there. In a 1971 meeting of the Baptist General Convention of Texas we heard the Christian testimony of one of the outstanding astronauts who explored the moon on the recent moon probe.

No, God was not taken by surprise when man, with his ever expanding knowledge, was able to put a spacecraft into orbit, send it to the moon, and miraculously return safely to this earth. Man has never gone anywhere beyond God's presence, God's providence and God's power. We've never touched the hem of the garment in God's creative ability. We don't begin to understand the secrets of the universe. We can't even grasp the distances represented in infinity out in space.

Perhaps in some ways God could be likened to a father

who holds a Ph.D. degree in mathematics. This father has a son who has just entered the first grade. He sees him come home at night with his arithmetic papers and watches him as he works tediously, laboriously. He sees the glee on the face of the little boy who figures out that two plus two equals four. I can imagine the father, with a Ph.D. in math, smiles indulgently, benignly, delighted that his son has grown to that point, but knowing that beyond are riches and depths that the boy could not begin to grasp now, but which one day he'll be able to uncover. When man with all of his vaunted prowess begins to touch the hem of the garment in the universe, Christians can sit back, smile and applaud and encourage man to continue in this venture, knowing full well that God is there, that he populated space long before he created mankind and that his holy angels are there in ranks, divisions, and organizations, doing the will of God and ministering to needs wherever they are. In his love and wisdom God is helping us to grasp more of the truth of the universe which he has created, and we need to understand that there are spiritual realities out there just as truly as there are material realities. Spiritual facts are discerned through God's revelation and through our continued study of his Word and an application of it.

3

THE PERSONALITY OF ANGELS

In preceding studies we have discussed the presence of angels, or the reality of them. This affirmed the fact that they exist, and we have underscored the truth that we believe in angels because the Bible teaches us about them, Jesus Christ believed in them, and Christ our Lord, the omniscient, omnipotent Son of God, told us that these ministering spirits would be present in our world.

Characteristically, the ministry of angels has been directed more toward the physical and material aspects of human life than the spiritual. This is a distinction we keep clearly in mind, for angels are not to be confused with the presence, the power, or the ministry of the Holy Spirit. The Holy Spirit is the Interpreter and Revealer of Jesus Christ. He's the One who elucidates the things of the spirit. He gives our minds understanding of things we could never grasp with carnal mind. The ministry of the Holy Spirit is separate and distinct from the ministry of angels. I want us to think about three things regarding the personality of angels. First their appearance, then their abode, and finally some attributes of angels. First, then, their

APPEARANCE

Hebrews 1:14 reminds us that angels are ministering

spirits. As such they are not visible to the human eye. There are cases in the Bible when the appearance of angels was so much like the appearance of men that they passed for men. People thought they were men. This was true with Lot in Sodom when visited by angels. They were so like humans that other humans thought they were people. They didn't understand who these men were. Obviously then, angels on occasion must bear characteristics similar to human beings. Now I say this with another verse of Scripture in mind, namely Hebrews 13:2. There we are admonished to entertain strangers because there's a possibility that we might entertain angels unawares. In other words, angels on occasion must bear characteristics entirely similar to our human bodies.

Now we don't have any indication that they have a long physical existence, that they have a natural birth or anything like this, but on occasion they have appeared in a form enough like that of humans to be thought to be human.

There are instances in which the appearance of angels is not connected with any characteristic of the human body, but they are seen in dazzling brilliance and blazing glory. In Matthew 28:2–4 we find such a record. There, angels appeared in dazzling brilliance. Now the conclusion in my mind is that angels possess the faculty of appearing in corporeal form, that is in bodily form, according to God's purpose. If God chooses, an angel can visit this earth with characteristics similar enough to our bodies to be mistaken for a human. On other occasions angels pierce the universe at a speed greater than the speed of light, and I believe they come and go unperceived by mortal sense, or they can appear visibly according to God's purpose. So if they appear in a form that we think is human, if we see or entertain an angel unawares, this is because of God's purpose. In the majority of cases angels are not perceived by human eyes.

I think it's interesting to make some comparisons between angels and Christians here on earth. There are some marked differences between them. First of all, an angel cannot call God "Father" by redemption. The holy angels never sinned, therefore have no need of salvation. They've never been saved because they've never sinned, and that's a marked difference. God is not their Father in the same sense in which he is your Father and mine, through the redemptive process and faith in Jesus Christ.

Secondly, angels are not indwelt by the Holy Spirit. The Holy Spirit does not motivate the life of an angel. He is not their prompter because the Holy Spirit is given to believers and comes in at the moment of conviction of sin and conversion from sin. Since the holy angels never sinned, the Holy Spirit does not indwell them.

A third thing: angels are not heirs of God. These heirs of God, those of us who fall into the family of God by redemption, are those who have heard and heeded salvation's story. We're the heirs of God for we are the ones to whom God promised the richest blessings of heaven. Heaven comes because of our repentance from sin and faith in the Lord Jesus Christ. The angels have never had this experience.

And then another closely associated difference: angels cannot witness to salvation. Have you ever stopped to think that this is a privilege God has given us that is denied even to angels? On certain nights we go out as a church, witnessing in our community and exercising a God-given privilege denied the angels in heaven and on earth. They don't have the privilege of witnessing to what God has done for them in salvation. The appearance of angels may be in a form similar to a body like yours and mine. If so, it's because of God's purpose. In the majority of instances angels are not corporeal, that is, encased in bodies, but they're invisible to the eye. Let's think for a moment about their

ABODE

As I discussed Mars, 78 million miles from earth, the Red Planet which had a dust storm, it occurred to one person that space scientists didn't have to go to Mars to find a dust storm. They could have hung around West Texas and caught up with one before long. They took pictures of a dust storm on Mars!

The point I tried to make is that we're not to confine our thinking in regard to the presence of angels to this terestrial ball. This earth is not the only place inhabited by angels. Out there in the vastness of infinity, beyond the comprehension of the human mind, beyond our ability to grasp, there are nevertheless ministering spirits called the angels of God. Their angelic abode is out there in the heavenlies as well as here on earth.

I stated previously that the universe is inhabited by innumerable hosts of angelic beings. Now in Mark 13:32 Jesus used the phrase, "the angels which are in heaven." That pretty firmly establishes their abode: they're in heaven. Jesus said it and we believe it. They inhabit the heavenly spheres. The apostle Paul in one of his epistles wrote: "Though an angel from heaven. . . ." Obviously, they inhabit the heavenlies. Again, in Ephesians 3:15, Paul wrote: "The whole family in heaven and in earth." Now, you'll recall that Christ taught his disciples to pray a prayer in which they were instructed to say: "Thy will be done on earth as it is in heaven." Quite obviously, the inhabitants of heaven who are doing the will of God are these ministering spirits standing at the beck and call of omnipotence, ready instantaneously to perform God's will, to do his service in the lives of human beings. Now we've said that the angels' abode is heavenly.

I want also to assert that the earthly ministry of angels is positively stated in the Word of God. Not only does the record reveal frequent visits of angels to our world as messengers of God, both to governments and individuals, but Jesus himself made reference to this fact. This is what I find in Luke 15:10, where Jesus said: "Likewise, I say unto you, there is joy in the presence of the angels of God over one sinner that repenteth." I take that as self-evident, attesting to the fact that angels are here and know when one sinner repents. Where are they? Where is their abode? They're out there in the eternities of the heavenlies, but they're also here on earth and aware of what's going on in your life and mine. When we turn from sin in repentance and receive Jesus Christ in faith, there is rejoicing in the presence of God, in the great angelic host, over the fact that down here on earth someone has turned from sin and has been redeemed.

Now I think that verse in Luke 15:10 points up that they're in close contact with everything going on in heaven and everything going on in earth. They understand the joy in the heart of God when a sinner repents, therefore they share that joy and express it in their exuberance.

Do you know that the entire fifteenth chapter of Luke deals with the joy of God in recovering a sinner? The three parables found there have to do with that joy. One of them is the parable of the lost sheep. Ninety-nine are safe in the fold, but there's one lost one. The shepherd, who in the parable is God, keeps on searching, keeps on looking until that last lost sheep has been found and brought to safety.

In the parable of the lost coin, God is like that woman who lost something valuable and does not cease her search until she finds it. That's the way God is. That's something we can understand of the yearning in the heart of God for the salvation of a lost sinner.

Then in the final parable, the joy of God is seen in the heart of the father, whose boy, the prodigal son, has gone a long way from home, who has sunk to the very depths of degradation and sin. But one day the boy comes to his senses and returns home, and when he does the father is overjoyed. The father called for the servants and said to bring forth the best robe (not some used one, not one that we're through with; bring the best we've got), bring a ring to put on his hand, and bring shoes to put on his feet, and have a banquet for this boy. "That's descriptive of the joy in the heart of God over a sinner who comes home. The angels of God are aware of that joy, and when a sinner repents they set all the joy bells of heaven in motion with their rejoicing. So the abode of angels is firmly established in the teachings of Jesus Christ as being both earthly and heavenly. Just as surely as there are angels praising God in worship daily in his eternal presence, there are angels ministering to human need here in this earth and rejoicing in the salvation of those who are saved. Now let's observe some angelic

ATTRIBUTES

What can we glean from the teachings of the Word of God about these who are called ministering spirits? Angels are individual beings. They're not a mass or a glob, they're individuals just like you and me, and apparently they experience emotion. In Psalm 148:2 we read that they render intelligent worship. Obviously, they possess emotions. In Matthew 18:10 we're taught that angels possess due understanding as they behold the face of the Father.

Another of the attributes of angels is that they understand or grasp their limitations. In Matthew 24:36 we read that they do not have all knowledge, for there are matters known to God not known by the angels. In Hebrews 1:4 we read that angels are inferior to Jesus Christ. He is above the angels.

As summation, let's recall these truths taught in the Bible regarding angels. First, they are created beings. God brought them into existence and as best we can understand they were created prior to the creation of mankind. According to the book of Job they were witnesses to the creation. According to Job they were the morning stars who sang before man was placed on the face of the earth. In Psalm 148:5 and in Colossians 1:16 we read that they are created beings. This reminds us that God alone is uncreated and eternal. His eternality is stated in 1 Timothy 3:16 where we read of God, "Who alone hath immortality."

There's a second thing we need to remember about angels. Angels are incorporeal, that is, without human bodies.

They're described in our text as spirits. When there is any deviation from this, it's for the purpose of fulfilling God's eternal plan. This implies that they have no bodies, for the Bible teaches us and Jesus has taught us they know nothing of growth, age, marriage, or death. They do not procreate themselves. Angels do not have children. There are the same number of angels today that there were when God originally created them. Since there's no death, since there's no procreation, there's neither an increase nor a decrease of the angelic hosts. Their number is the same, understanding that there was a defection among angels, in which the angels who sinned fell from their original, holy estate.

A third thing. Angels possess personality. By that I mean that they are intelligent, voluntary beings. They can render intelligent worship such as we find described in Psalm 148:2, so certainly we understand that, as intelligent beings, they are personalities. They're voluntary also, just as you and I, else Lucifer would have had no choice between right and wrong. He chose sin as a result of his pride. He was the leader of the fallen angels, whom we also call demons. They are aligned with Satan and are the power and force of hell. They're in constant opposition to the holy angels, to the power of God, and to the influence and might of God's Holy Spirit. In 2 Samuel 14:20 we read, ". . . wise, according to the wisdom of an angel of God." So they possess personalities. They have intelligence, and they have a voluntary spirit. They can choose right or wrong just as can you and I.

A fourth attribute. They are intelligent beings, but their intelligence is superhuman, as is their power. When I say superhuman, I don't mean omnipotent. Their power, their intelligence, is between that of ours and that of God. Superhuman—greater than humans—but not equal, not greater than the power and knowledge of almighty God. There are things they don't know. For instance, the angels do not know the time of the second coming of Christ. First Peter 1:12 indicates the desire of angels to look into some things that are unknown. Psalm 103:20, a very important verse, points out that angels are mighty in strength. Second Thessalonians 1:7 refers to the angels of his power. In Revelation 20:2 and 10 we're told that it is the angels of God who'll lay hold upon the dragon and bind him and cast him into the lake of fire. That dragon is Satan or Lucifer, a fallen angel who rebelled against God in his pride. God's angels will bind Satan and cast him into that place of eternal punishment.

What can we say then about the attributes of angels? We can say that power, rather than beauty or even intelligence, is their outstanding mark. They're better known for their power than anything else. Recall that it was angels, who, in their power rolled away the stone from in front of the tomb where Jesus Christ was laid after his crucifixion. Those who have been there and have seen the Garden Tomb, and have seen that trough in which the stone was rolled back, can well understand that we're talking about a block of granite that may well have weighed four tons. The angels of God rolled away that stone from the tomb and Jesus came forth alive.

It is the ministry of angels in your life and in mine to help and strengthen. Since they are God's messengers, they minister in response to his command, and I believe that they are available to us in the fulfilment of our prayers in the will of God every minute of every day.

4

THE PURPOSES OF ANGELS

Hebrews 12:1

In a book published over a hundred years ago, Richard Whateley made this statement: "Any person or any thing may be employed by the Lord to do his will—to convey his message to men or to perform any service for them. And whoever or whatever is employed becomes God's angel or messenger. Whether a supernatural flame (Moses and the burning bush out of which God spoke) or any other appearance, or any voice from heaven, or any other personal agent of a different nature from man—whatever or whoever holds communion with mankind is called his angels or his messengers." Now that's a broad statement and inclusive. I believe, however, the more you think about it the more prone you'll be to agree with it.

God has used many different messengers to convey his truths to the minds and hearts of men. The service God performs in the interest of human beings is performed in a wide variety of ways. So this author, over a hundred years ago, was simply saying God can choose any method he wishes to perform his service in the lives of human beings.

The faithful service of angels to mankind is not based on their love for you and me. It's based on their love for God, and they respond to the wishes of God in their ministry to us. If God would give his only begotten Son to die for a lost race of men, angels will follow suit as far as possible and at least give instant service for his sake wherever it is appointed unto them.

Now it's not imagination but reality that angels are servants of men in thousands of ways. Hebrews 1:14, to which we have frequently referred, states it in this way: "Are they not all ministering spirits, sent forth to minister for them who shall be heirs of salvation?" Of course that includes a ministry to the church, for those who comprise the true church are the heirs of salvation. Angels are serving the community of the redeemed, and in a study to follow we'll consider several ways in which angels minister directly to the church.

From the Old Testament you recall the experience of Jacob. In a dream, a vision, he saw a ladder stretching from heaven to earth, and on that ladder angels ascending and descending. Now I believe that the dream, or vision, Jacob had is as true today as it was in his day, for the pathway is still open; and in the purpose of Jesus Christ these heavenly messengers come bearing gifts and succor from the Bridegroom to his distressed and lonely Bride, the church. It is the ministry of angels in the church that gives us the supply of our need when it seems that all doors have been closed. Just as the angels are servants of Christ, so they serve the church.

I want to center now on three aspects of their ministry. These are purposes, as I understand it, for which God created angels and by which he uses them in our lives and our world. Their first purpose is the purpose of them in our lives and our world. Their first purpose is the purpose

PRAISE

There's an important insight in Revelation 5:11 f. "And I beheld," John wrote, "and I heard the voice of many angels round about the throne and the beasts and the elders; and the number of them was ten thousand times ten thousand and thousands of thousands; Saying with a loud voice, Worthy is the Lamb. . . ." Probably the most prominant truth that jumps out of this passage is the number of angels. I don't believe this is any more to be taken literally than the words of Jesus to Simon Peter when he asked the Lord, "How many times should I forgive?" Jesus said, "Not seven times, but seventy times seven." He was saying that Simon Peter should live in an aura of forgiveness. Don't keep count. Don't add up every time you've forgiven. Just keep on forgiving and forgiving and forgiving. Now here we have numbers that I also believe are symbolic, for I'm not convinced that the number of angels is literally ten thousand times ten thousand, plus these thousands of thousands. I think they are an innumerable host. They are beyond counting.

In this passage we ask what these angels are doing. The answer is, they are praising God. They are magnifying what Jesus did for mankind. They're standing around the throne crying out, "Worthy is the Lamb." In other words, what Jesus did is altogether worthy, completely, and totally acceptable.

I think it's also interesting to note that these angels are not said to be singing. How many times have you heard about the angelic choir? We don't have much indication in the New Testament that they're going to sing. They're praising God. It may be in song, but it may not be. In fact, the clearest indication we have of musical talent on the part of an angel is when an angel will sound the trumpet of God. He's going to blow a horn, sound a trumpet, marking the Second Coming of Jesus Christ.

These angels standing around the throne are verbally praising God saying "Worthy is the Lamb." That means they are stating that he is altogether acceptable. What he has done is completely approved and he is worthy to receive the praise and the adulation of mankind. These angels are gathered to extol the virtues of Jesus Christ, to state the characteristics that were displayed in his life here on earth and to praise God for these virtues.

I think there's a lesson here we ought to learn. A very vital part of our worship, like that of angels who stand in the presence of God, should be to praise his Name and state our commitment to his worthiness and faithfulness.

The estate of the angels, just like your estate and mine, is based on God's faithfulness. They are who they are because God is who he is. We are who we are, sinners saved by the grace of God through faith in Jesus Christ, because God is faithful. A very vital part of our worship ought to be to praise his holy name for his faithfulness in doing what he said he would do.

Again, the prophet Isaiah had a great vision of God's glory, recorded in Isaiah 6. The angels there are heard repeating one word: "Holy." "Holy, holy, holy" is the praise that the angels are giving in the vision of Isaiah. That word means sanctified, separated, set apart, unique, different. That's exactly true when it comes to our worship of God, for he is altogether different. He's different from us, and he's different from any other object of worship man might ever devise. "Holy, Holy, Holy!" I like the song we sing which bears that title. Ordinarily we sing it on Sunday mornings: "Holy, holy, holy, Lord God almighty." When we sing that hymn and mean it, we are praising God in something of the same way angels praise God. We state his virtues, his characteristics, and we thank him for them.

If it were not for God's faithfulness, you and I would be lost. If it were not for God's love, he never would have sent Christ to redeem us from our sins.

Think of the different characteristics of God! Those are the virtues we ought to extol and magnify when we gather in worship. We are who we are because he is who he is. One of the purposes of angels is praise. There's another. This purpose is to

PROTECT

Many of you recall the cherubim in the book of Genesis. These are angelic beings. (The word "cherubim" is the plural of cherub.) In the book of Genesis we find these angels. They are seen as sentinels protecting the Garden of Eden after man had been driven out.

It was the mercy of God that placed the cherubim in that position of protection. Within the Garden of Eden there was not only the tree of the knowledge of good and evil from which Adam and Eve ate, there was also the tree of life in the center of the Garden. If Adam and Eve, after having eaten of the fruit of the tree of knowledge of good and evil, had returned to the Garden after their banishment and had stolen fruit from the tree of life, it would surely have resulted in awesome disaster. If man had eaten from that tree he would have lived forever in his bodily estate, and thus he would have prolonged his miserable existence on earth in sin, sickness, pain, and sorrow endlessly.

I want to remind you of a distinction that needs to be made here. Immortality was not lost when man sinned. Man did not lose the image of God, which is the spark of eternality God gives every human being. Genesis 3:22 has to do with the body and not the soul. Because of man's sin, he lost the privilege of continued bodily existence. So the angels of God, the cherubim, were placed as guards to keep man from returning to the Garden of Eden, that pelucid paradise of God, and eating of the tree of life which would mean that the earthly body would have continued to exist indefinitely.

In Daniel we find this protective ministry of angels clearly revealed. After the servant of God named Daniel had been cast into the lion's den, he was uniquely protected. In Daniel 6:22 we read: "My God hath sent his angel, and hath shut the lions' mouths." That's the protective ministry of angels. When man has no other recourse, when he's in a predicament because of his belief in God and his witness for God, God provides unique protection.

We find this again in Acts 12:15, where the apostle Peter was uniquely protected by an angel. He was awakened from a deep sleep, his shackles were loosed, and he was led out of prison. Can you imagine Simon Peter sleeping on the night before he was to be killed? He was in prison as a part of the persecution of Christians being carried out by Herod Agrippa, the grandson of Herod the Great. This sadistic ruler, who had already put James to death, was now beginning a systematic persecution of Christians in Jerusalem. Simon Peter was taken prisoner and placed in prison. He was told his life would be exacted. Rather than fretting, cracking his knuckles, wringing his hands, and bemoaning his fate, when they left him alone in that cell he went to sleep so soundly the angel had to jab him in the side to wake him up.

Some ladies have an angelic ministry in church. You go right ahead and nudge that fellow and keep him awake. When he starts to go to sleep, let him have it! And then when he turns and looks at you, he ought to call you angel, because you're doing what an angel did on another occasion. The protective ministry of angels in the lives of believers is clear. Redeemed sinners, washed in the blood of Christ, are the glory of Christ. Just as angels minister to our Savior, so they minister to those who belong to him.

Keep in mind that there are hostile forces in the world. According to the Bible, "the world lieth in the wicked one." The Devil is stated to be the "prince of the powers of this world" and the Devil hates Jesus Christ. He is an active murderer and liar, trying in every way at his disposal to thwart the purposes of God. Though Christ has established his ultimate power, and though he has once and for all broken Satan's hold, nevertheless the Devil attacks any who name that Name, which is above every name. He hates Christ and those who are followers of Christ. If Satan could, he would end the life of every child of God on earth. The reason he's not effective in his effort is because of the ministry and protective care of God's angels. The true church is the object of the Devil's hatred.

On the other hand, the angels of God are ministering to God's children in the midst of all of Satan's attacks. Now I want to suggest a third purpose. The purpose of angels are to praise, to protect, and to

PUNISH

Think once more of the incident recorded in Acts 12:20. Herod Agrippa, a pompous, vainglorious individual, received the adulation of the people. They exclaimed, when they heard him speak, that his voice was the voice of a god and not the voice of man. Immediately an angel of God smote him, because he gave not God the glory, and he was eaten by worms and gave up the ghost. What happened to him? God's angel punished him!

The text is not as explicit in the case of Ananias and Sapphira, but in light of this incident in Acts the twelfth chapter, I believe that's what happened to Ananias and Sapphira. They dared to lie to God, and when they did, they both died. Here an angel was used to bring God's punishment.

In Matthew 13:39 f. there is another illustration. Jesus said the end of the world will be like a harvest and the reapers of that harvest will be angels. Jesus said it! He said he would "send forth his angels, and they shall gather out of his kingdom all things that offend, and them which do iniquity; And shall cast them into a furnace of fire: there shall be wailing and gnashing of teeth." Now who's going to do this? The angels of God. How they'll do it, I don't know. But Jesus said they'd be responsible for this. They will extract from the kingdom the tares from the wheat, the goats from the sheep, and they'll cast them into everlasting punishment. The angels will be agents of God in judgment, bringing about the punishment of the unsaved.

Keep in mind that this punishment will not come because of sins, plural, but the punishment of the unsaved will come as the result of sin, singular. The sin for which one goes to an everlasting hell is the sin of rejecting Jesus Christ. One doesn't go to hell because he is a murderer; there are murderers in heaven. David the King was one such, and I'm sure that there are innumerable others. I'm not advocating murder, but I'm saying that sins, plural, do not cause a person to go to hell. One sin sends a man to everlasting destruction, and one act of will brings a man into eternal bliss in a place called heaven. Rejecting Jesus sends a man to hell, and accepting Jesus assures one of heaven. The only avenue of escape from punishment for the unsaved is faith in the Lord Jesus Christ. The only way we can escape punishment for sin, singular, is to repent of that sin we've committed, the sin of trying to do it ourselves, the sin of standing on our own, the sin of doing it our way, and in repentance turn to Jesus Christ to receive what he offers us.

The most vital question you'll ever face is, "What will you do with Jesus?" That's the question that faces you right now, and it's one no one can answer for you. You must answer it yourself. What will you do with Jesus?

You may do one of two things, and there is no other alternative. You either accept him or reject him. Our Lord himself said, "He that is not with me is against me, and he that gathereth not with me, scattereth abroad." You're the one who makes the determination as to whose side you are on. If you will accept Jesus, if you'll trust him, if you'll stand for him openly, if you'll confess him before men, you can make that commitment at this moment. We'll rejoice with you and even the angels in heaven will rejoice over one sinner who repents.

5

YOUR PERSONAL ANGEL

Matthew 18:10

From an overall viewpoint, and on the basis of our study to this point, it seems that in the Old Testament angels were sensible manifestations of Jehovah God. They made an appearance recognizable by human beings. They appeared to be human in some cases, such as in the case of Lot, who entertained angels. On occasion the angelic manifestation was in the visible form of a flame, such as with Moses and the burning bush, or maybe some other emblem visible to the human eye.

In the New Testament, however, angels appear to be personal agents. There's a wide difference of opinion among scholars as to whether or not there are personal, or guardian, angels. Many scholars laugh at the idea. Others believe it with all the conviction of their hearts. It is my judgment that we cannot accept the Bible as God's inspired Word and discount the reality of personal angels. I believe the truth is clear, and that an understanding of it must be had if we're to experience the Christian life in its fullest and finest.

There are particular incidents in the New Testament where angels of God ministered to the personal, individual need of one of God's children. I believe in a personal angel, not just in these specific New Testament instances, but for all of us who are children of God. The writer of Hebrews reminds us that angels are "ministering spirits," given the responsibility of ministering to those of us who have been saved, who have been born into the family of God. I'm convinced that you and I both have a personal angel. Let's note the personal ministry of angels in three directions. First of all in deliverance, then in danger, and finally in death.

DELIVERANCE

In our text we are told that angels behold the face of the Father in heaven. Now recall this entire passage, beginning where we began in the second verse of the eighteenth chapter. Jesus was answering a question that had been put to him regarding who is greatest in the kingdom of heaven. He put a little child in the midst of the group and stated to all gathered around that unless we be converted—that is, unless we turn—repent, and be born again, and become like a little child, we cannot enter into the kingdom.

In a real sense Jesus is talking about chronological children, children from the standpoint of their age; but as we read this passage we also become convinced that he refers to believers. He is not just talking about a two- or three- or five-year-old. He is talking about little children in the kingdom of God in regard to their understanding and spiritual maturity. A new Christian may be an adult physically, but at the moment of his conversion he becomes a babe in Christ. Jesus obviously referred to these babes in Christ in what he was saying.

The offenses of the kingdom are not just offenses toward

little children. I don't know many people who spend their time trying to offend little children. Most of us love them. Once in a while you'll find in a church a person who is incensed at the actions of children, but mostly they are people whose children are grown and gone or who have never had any children. I don't know many people who go around trying to hurt little kids. Most of us love them.

On the other hand, it is far easier to offend a little child in spiritual understanding, though that one may be fifty or sixty years of age. It is an easy thing, if we are not very careful, to become offensive in our influence and lead such a little one astray. I think Jesus included that caution in this verse of Scripture.

I think this would also include every college professor who, by design or simply by failure to give attention to his responsibility, offends and misdirects a young person who is earnestly seeking to know and to do God's will. I think such a person is included in this condemnation. If there be such in seminaries, I would say they also would be included. It is far better for a millstone to be hanged around the neck of such a one and he be drowned in the depth of the sea than offend one of these little ones. The little one may be grown physically, but in spiritual understanding still may be a child.

In verse 5 Jesus is not referring just to chronological children, but to the child of the kingdom. In verse 6 he also refers to the kingdom citizen. In verse 10, in the same thinking and context, he refers to little ones who have their angels in the presence of the Father. So I think he talks about Christians here. Some of us are still little ones in understanding, and I believe he implies that we have angels who stand in the presence of the Father and who know our needs.

Psalm 91:11 is a verse that's well known to all of us, a verse that the devil used in trying to tempt our Lord. However, we must understand that Psalm 91 is not considered a Messianic Psalm. This Psalm was not prophetic of the coming of Jesus Christ. It rather has reference to all of us. Now certainly it does refer to Jesus, but not in an exclusive, specific sense. The Devil said in essence to Jesus: "Why don't you climb to the pinnacle of the Temple and jump? Before you hit the ground the angels will bear you up least you dash your foot against the stone." That verse also includes us as believers in Jesus Christ.

Take another verse, Psalm 34:7, "The angel of the Lord encampeth round about them that fear him, and delivereth them." Now that's why I say we can see the ministry of our personal angels in deliverance. This is one of the tasks which God has assigned to your personal angel and mine.

In Daniel 6:22 we read: "My God hath sent his angel, and hath shut the lions' mouths." Daniel understood that his deliverance was of God, and it came through a personal angelic ministry. God's angel kept those lions from devouring his flesh.

Another incident of deliverance attributed to angels is found in Acts 12:6 ff. Simon Peter had a miraculous deliverance from prison. When he went to knock on the door of the home where the Christians were meeting in prayer for him, one came to the door and was so excited and so amazed that she returned to the group without unlocking the door; and cried, the group decided that it was Peter's angel. It was Simon Peter himself. He was delivered by an angel of God. Now we see the ministry of your personal angel in deliverance from these biblical illustrations; but let's think about your personal angel in a time of

DANGER

Men of God in every generation can witness to miraculous escapes from threatening dangers that are unexplainable in any other way but the providential ministry of God. The greatest proof that I know of the reality of guardian angels is that some of you are alive, the way you drive an automobile. If it were not for the angelic provision for your safety, you wouldn't be here. I include myself in that category on occasions.

Charles Wesley wrote about angels: "Angels wher'er we go, attend our steps what'er betide, With watchful care their charge defend, and evil turn aside." Charles Wesley had a conviction about personal angels.

There's an interesting record from the life of the apostle Paul in Acts 27. On the way to Rome to be tried before Caesar, he was involved in a shipwreck. It was an angel of God who brought the message to Paul that there was hope. He announced to the 275 others on board ship that not a one of them would be lost. He reported that an angel of God had revealed this to him. His personal angel was ministering to his physical needs and protecting him in a time of danger. In 27:23 Paul stated, "For there stood by me this night the angel of God."

I suppose every Christian here can witness to the miraculous preservation of life in a time of danger. I look back across my life and see many instances where I was providentially spared injury or maybe death. I remember one occasion when I was a student at Mercer University. It was ninety miles from my hometown in Newnan down to Macon where Mercer is located. At one time during my four-year stay, there were eighteen young people from our home church enrolled in Mercer. Several of them had well-to-do parents, and they had their own automobiles. You can imagine that we drove back and forth together. I ordinarily rode with a young fellow, a good friend of mine, named Art Fuller. I can't tell you to this day why I was not with him on a certain Sunday afternoon return trip. After lunch I told Dad that if he would drive me out to the Griffin highway, I thought I would just hitchike back and get back to school a little early. I knew Art and the others that would ride with him wouldn't leave until five or six o'clock and would get back to Macon at eight or eight-thirty, and I wanted to get back earlier than that. And for some reason, and I never did tell him that I wasn't going to ride with him, I got a ride out to the forks of the road and put my thumb in the air and went on back to school. That night the phone rang and I learned that Art and the others in his car had been involved in a very serious automobile accident down near Turin, which was about eighteen miles from home, and that all of them were in the hospital—broken bones, lacerations, cuts, contusions, concussions, and they were all seriously injured. If there had been one more person in the car, there probably would have been a loss of life by the way the impact came—a head-on collision. I don't know any reason why I was not in that car except the providence of God.

I don't believe there's a person reading this but who

could relate some similar story. You've seen the hand of God in your life in a miraculous way, delivering you from danger. Our very lives today, our existence, our presence here are testimonies to God's providential and supernatural protection. Now there's one other word that I want to add regarding the ministry of our personal angels:

DEATH

A familiar story from the life of our Lord is recorded in Luke 16:20 f. Scholars have called this a parable. Our Lord did not so state. Jesus did not say, "I am telling you a parable." Luke, the author, did not write, "I am relating a parable Jesus told," as Luke did on occasion, such as in Luke 18:1, where he wrote: "He spake a parable unto them to this end, that men ought always to pray, and not to faint." "He spake a parable." There is no indication that Luke 16:20 f. is a parable. In a true parable Jesus Christ never named the names of persons involved. Think for a moment. He would say when speaking in parables, "A sower went forth to sow." Now what was his name? He didn't use a name. He said, "A wise man builded his house upon a rock," but he did not name the wise man. When speaking in parables Jesus did not identify people.

In Luke 16 the persons involved are identified by name and by state. In this story the poor man is named Lazarus. The name *Lazarus* means "God is my help," and that's the point of the story. This poor man stationed himself outside the gate of the wealthy man. He was dependent upon the wealthy man. His food consisted of the scraps thrown from the table of the rich man after he had eaten all he wanted. The rich man's dog came and licked the sores of the poor man who was outside the gate. In the parable (verse 22) we find a contrast between the death of Lazarus, whose name means "God is my help," and Dives, who was the rich man. When Lazarus died, he was carried by the angels into Abraham's bosom. Now is that a parable? Is that concocted out of the figment of Christ's imagination to illustrate a point and prove a particular truth? I think it's a story taken from life, representing real people and a real situation.

Lazarus was escorted into the presence of God by the holy angels. What a wonderful comforting truth! Friends, that's Scripture, and I believe it. I believe when a child of God dies, in the moment, in the split second life ceases in his body, and the spirit made in the image of God rejoins the Father, that spirit will be escorted into the presence of almighty God by your personal angel and possibly others, rejoicing in the glorious graduation day you have achieved, and escorting you into the presence of God with the greatest and highest joy.

A songwriter put it like this: "I won't have to cross Jordan alone, Jesus died for my sins to atone." So when that last moment comes and we step across chilly Jordan, we won't be alone. Our personal angel will see to it that we're brought into the presence of our Creator and Redeemer, to be presented to him with all joy, and there will never be a moment in eternity when we will be alone.

This ought to give great comfort to every Christian to know that when death comes, immediately we'll be in the presence of angels and of God. In 2 Corinthians 5:8 Paul wrote, "We are confident, I say, and willing rather to be absent from the body, and to be present with the Lord."

Just that quickly, absent from the body, present with the Lord. When that moment of physical and spiritual separation takes place, the angels will escort us into the presence of our Savior and we'll be united with him and all the heirs of salvation forever and forever.

6

ANGELIC PROVISION FOR JESUS CHRIST

Matthew 4:11

In Hebrew 12:22 reference is made to an "innumerable company of angels." In the Greek this is the word for "myriad," and it actually means tens of thousands. So when we talk about the angelic host, we are talking about tens of thousands, an innumerable company, far greater than the mind of man can ever count or grasp.

The Bible teaches that angels are spirits, but there are numerous instances in the Bible where they've taken on visible bodies, or physical manifestations. Our text indicates that angels ministered to Jesus Christ. I think an interesting sideline here is the Greek verb translated "ministered." It is the verb *diakoneo*. Now some of you who have heard me preach recently might remember that verb. It is the same root from which we get our word deacon. *Diakoneo*—the word means to be a servant, an attendant, a domestic, to serve or to wait upon. Remember then that these angels performed a function comparable to the function of a deacon. That ought to be a challenge and inspiration to every ordained deacon. These angels, or heavenly deacons, came to minister to the Son of God in a time of distress and need. Let's see the angelic ministry to Jesus Christ in three ways: First in preparation; then in provision; and finally in prophecy. First in

PREPARATION

Recall these instances that took place prior to the coming of Christ as the way was being prepared for his coming. There was an aged priest, a righteous man in whose heart burned brightly the flame of hope for the coming of Messiah. That priest was named Zacharias, which means, "the Lord remembers." His wife was named Elizabeth and that name means "God's oath." One day Zacharias the priest was burning incense in the Temple while all of the people outside stood and prayed. As Zacharias officiated an angel of the Lord appeared unto him on the right side of the altar and spoke. The angel announced to this priest the coming of one who would be the forerunner of the Messiah, John the Baptist. He stated this one would come as the son of this priest and his wife.

That same angel, Gabriel, next comes from the throne of God to a little city called Nazareth. You can find this incident recorded in Luke 1:19 and 26. This is the same angel we find 600 years earlier, as recorded in Daniel 9:24–27, who announced when Christ would suffer. The first word of the angel Gabriel to Zacharias was, "Fear not."

The first word of this angel to Mary, the virgin, was "Hail." That word literally means, "Oh, joy." When Gabriel announced to Mary that she would give birth to this Child, he said at the very outset, "Oh, joy!" I imagine that was an expression of the feeling, the emotion, of Gabriel, for he had known for millenia that this great and glorious day would come. Now he had the incomparable privilege of preparing the way through making the announcement to Mary, the earthly mother of Jesus Christ.

Angels were witnesses to the creative act of God when he made the first man, Adam, out of the dust of the earth. Keep Adam in your mind. The angel saw God as he created Adam. Then angels witnessed the creative act of God when he brought into being the second Man, Jesus Christ. In the first man, Adam, all sinned and all die. In the second Man, Jesus Christ, all who put their faith and trust in him are made alive again and forevermore. So angels witnessed the whole broad scope of the creative power of God and his consummate acts of power in bringing forth man's escape from sin and the penalty thereof. Jesus Christ was conceived in the womb of the virgin Mary by the Holy Spirit, and as a result of his birth, all of those who would die in Adam have the opportunity to be made alive forevermore in Jesus Christ.

Then God's holy angel, having appeared unto Zacharias and Mary, next appeared unto Joseph. Joseph was a righteous, tender-hearted man. We find this record in Matthew 1:19 f. He was unwilling to embarrass Mary by breaking their engagement. The angel appeared to Joseph and said, "Fear not to take unto thee Mary thy wife." He obeyed the angel's command. Then came that momentous occasion. The Child of Prophecy came. All heaven was excited, for they knew what was taking place. They had looked forward with greatest anticipation to the moment when God would reveal himself in human form and would open the gates of glory to all who would enter through faith in the Lord Jesus Christ.

Now earth, at the time of the coming of Christ, was ignorant of this event, so an angel of the Lord appeared to shepherds watching their sheep. The glorious message to them was: "Fear not, for behold I bring you good tidings of great joy which shall be to all people. For unto you is born this day in the City of David, a Saviour, who is Christ the Lord. And this shall be a sign unto you. . . ." They went on making their announcement of what God was doing in the barn in Bethlehem. When the shepherds looked up, this one lone angel who initially appeared was joined by many, many others. So many in fact that they were called a vast host, a multitude of angels, all of whom were praising God.

Here is an interesting sidelight. We talk about the angelic chorus. Most of the time we assume that they sang. I cannot find a verse of Scripture that tells us the angels sang. I find where they praised God, where they did it verbally, but don't think just because you can sing that you're angelic. That may or may not be the case. There's no indication that I have found that they sang. Now if you can find a place where it says the angels sang, let me know. Remember in Isaiah there is a picture of the cherubim. They're said to be standing before the throne. They're praising God, but it doesn't say anything about singing. I don't know but that they might heist a tune every now and then, but there's no indication of it in the pages of the Book. It says they praised God, but it does not say that they sang.

The angels had waited for this glorious event all through the millenia since their creation by the hand of God. God gave the angels the glorious privilege of sharing in the preparation for the coming of the Redeemer. So we see this angelic ministry in preparation for the coming of Christ. Now let's notice the ministry of angels in their

PROVISION

for Jesus Christ. During his infancy, angels protected Jesus from physical harm. In Matthew 2:13 the angels who overshadowed Jesus Christ, the baby, warned Joseph to flee from the wrath of Herod into Egypt, and the angels directed the flight to safety. Remember, I have said that in my judgment the ministry of angels is physical, and that's what distinguishes their ministry from the ministry of the Holy Spirit. They were overseeing the physical safety and supplying the physical needs of Jesus Christ. I believe that's their ministry to you and me today. They do not usurp the spiritual ministry of the Holy Spirit. Their ministry is separate and distinct, and we have no indication in the Bible that their ministries overlap. The ministry of angels is physical; the ministry of the Holy Spirit is spiritual.

The next record of the provision of the angels for Jesus Christ comes at the time of our text. Just after our Lord had embarked on his earthly ministry, he was led up into the wilderness by the Spirit to be tempted of the Devil. He went forty days and forty nights fasting and praying and resisting the onslaughts of hell. When it was over and the Devil left him for a season—keep in mind that the Devil didn't leave him for good—the Devil didn't wash his hands of him and say he'll never have another problem from him; but the Devil just left him for a season. When he did, the angels came and ministered to his depleted physical resources.

In Luke 22:43 we find Jesus in the garden of Gethsemane. His soul is in such travail that his very blood is being squeezed out of him in the form of perspiration. There an angel came and made available to Jesus Christ the resources of heaven in his hour of physical distress. While hanging on Calvary's tree, legions of angels stood ready to be dispatched at an instant's notice, so undoubtedly angels were witnesses to the most dastardly deed ever perpetrated by human beings. When Christ was crucified on Calvary, all of the vast hosts of angels, that innumerable company, stood by helplessly and watched Jesus die.

Jesus said he could have called legions of angels to come to his rescue. They could have obliterated all of his enemies. Just as the death angel in the Old Testament came and slew the firstborn, so the angel of God in vengeance and wrath could have obliterated all of the enemies of Jesus Christ from the face of the earth. But Jesus never called for them. He could have called ten thousand angels, but he didn't. They could not come because they were not called for, and had they come God's plan of redemption would never have been complete.

The angels then saw the body of Jesus Christ placed in the tomb, and an angel was present to announce the resurrection of Jesus Christ from the dead and roll away the stone from the door of the tomb (Matt. 28:2, 3).

Again, in Acts 1:10–11, angels gave counsel to the disciples at the moment of Christ's ascension into heaven. When he left the Mount of Ascension, which is close by the Mount of Olives, angels appeared and spoke to the men of Galilee reminding them: "Ye men of Galilee, why stand ye gazing up into heaven? this same Jesus . . . shall so come in like manner as ye have seen him go into heaven." And so they encouraged those discouraged apostles who had seen Jesus Christ disappear into nothingness from their view. The angels reminded them they had a task to do, and that the Christ who was here is coming back. Now, all that we've discussed up to this point in the angelic provision for Jesus Christ has already been accomplished. This is not speculation. This is not an interpretation of the Word of God. This is a statement of what the Bible says concerning the ministry of angels to our Lord. But let's think for a moment about some events that have not yet transpired and see their ministry in

PROPHECY

Angels figure prominently in the second coming of Christ. In Matthew 25:31 we read: "When the Son of man shall come in his glory, and all the holy angels with him, then shall he sit upon the throne of his glory." In other words, when Jesus returns it will be to accompaniment of all the hosts of heaven. All the holy angels will be with him.

Now again in Matthew 13:41–42, we read that at the time of the second coming; "The Son of man shall send forth his angels, and they shall gather out of his kingdom all things that offend, and them which do iniquity; And shall cast them into a furnace of fire; there shall be wailing and gnashing of teeth." If you'll back up to verse 30 in that same thirteenth chapter, you'll find Jesus saying: "Let both [that is, the tares and the wheat, the bad and the good] grow together until the harvest: and in the time of harvest

I will say to the reapers, "Gather ye together first the tares, and bind them in bundles to burn them: but gather the wheat into my barn."

Some of the most perplexing theological questions that are addressed to me have to do with "Why doesn't God do so and so?" Usually it has to do with "Why doesn't God stop war? Why doesn't God remove and eliminate prejudice? Why does God permit evil in our world? Why doesn't God give a cure for cancer? Why doesn't God do this and this and this and this?" I can give you the answer right here in this text. Jesus said, "Let both grow together," the evil and the good. Now if he were to start wiping off the face of the earth all evil and he were to begin at midnigh tonight, how many of you think you would be here a 12:01? You had better thank God that he does not eliminate and remove all evil from the world, because if he did he would have to remove you and me along with it. Thank God he's going to let it all grow together, and then those of us who do know him will be gathered as wheat into his barn. The angels are the ones who do the gathering.

This truth is further substantiated in Matthew 24:31. "And he shall send his angels with a great sound of a trumpet, and shall gather together his elect from the four winds, from one end of heaven to the other."

Now there is another passage we will study in a chapter yet to come that points out that God has one of his angels stationed at each of the four corners of the earth. You say the earth is round. No, it's not exactly round. Scientists, geologists, and others have pointed out in recent years that there are four prominent places on the earth that very well could be called the four corners of the earth, standing as they do in the geographical position they occupy. So the Old Testament is not wrong after all! God has an angel stationed at each of the four corners of the earth.

Angels have an additional role in eschatology, for in Revelation 12:7 we read that Satan and his angels were cast out of heaven into the earth. Brother, if you want to know where the Devil is, I'll tell you! He's here. He's right here amongst us! He mixes it with us every day. He is the fallen angel, along with all of the other evil angels who, because of their sin, were cast out of heaven. They're here on this earth. They are fighting in your life and mine every day trying to win a victory that will challenge Christ. They're here.

The only time angels did not minister to our Savior was when he was on the Cross. He suffered alone for our sins. He could have called down the wrath of heaven upon his enemies, but for our sake he didn't. He knew that in the end, when he returns to this earth in power, right will be vindicated. The angels whom he could have called will in that day do his express bidding, and seal the victory once and for all against Satan, or Lucifer, the fallen angel, and all of those who are aligned with him. In the last days, according to the book of the Revelation, Satan, a fallen angel, will be bound and cast into that place of eternal torment, the lake that burneth with fire and brimstone. Ultimately, angels are seen in their eternal relationship with that city which comes down out of heaven from God, described in Revelation 21:9 ff.

When he was here on earth, the animals of the field

honored our Lord, for they moved over and allowed him to use their habitat. The fishes of the sea paid his taxes, the dove of peace crowned him at his baptism. Winds and waves were silent at his command. Trees died under his curse, and water blushed into wine at his command. All creation has joined together to honor our Lord—with one exception. That one exception is wicked, rebellious, covetous mankind. We are the only ones to whom he has given the power of choice. We are the only ones to whom he has given the eternality we possess, and we are the only ones who dare to rise up in rebellion, shake our fists in the face of God, and say: I'll do it my way." Can we be so callous? Can we be so wicked? Day by day he loves us, yearns for our redemption, and wants more than anything to give us the joy that he provides when we know and do his will.

7

A PROFILE OF ANGELS

Psalm 103:20

There are several scriptural indications that angels are organized. One of these is found in Jude 9 where reference is made to the archangel. The prefix "arch" means ruler. The archangel is the ruler of angels. Again, in the twenty-sixth chapter of the Gospel of Matthew, verse 53, Jesus referred to twelve legions of angels. Again that suggests some definite organization. So we do well to know that this innumerable host that transcends our ability to count, that far exceeds our imagination, is definitely organized and the purpose of their organization is to do the will of God explicitly. Look first at a number of

CATEGORIES

of angels. We find mentioned in the pages of God's Word: seraphim, cherubim, thrones, dominions, mights, powers, principalities, archangel, and angels. There are at least eight different Greek words used in the New Testament to designate these. In Colossians 1:16 we find a reference to thrones, lordships, principalities and authorities. In Romans 8:37 we find angels, principalities, and powers. In Ephesians 6:12 principalities, authorities, world rulers, and spiritual powers are named. There is some similarity and overlapping in these designations, but undoubtedly all of these refer to great dignity in varying degrees of rank.

One author commented that if God were to send an angel into this world to sweep the streets and another angel to occupy a position of regnancy on a throne, they would come without any equivocation and would receive identical joy simply through doing God's bidding. So these categories imply divisions among the angels and probably for a specific reason. God's will is carried out in one area by one category and in another area by another category of angels. Let's look more closely at two of these categories.

First, the seraphim. The only mention of these seraphim in the Bible is in Isaiah 6. He describes them well. They possess six wings, and in the vision Isaiah had, these seraphim covered their faces with two wings, they covered their feet with two wings, and with two remaining wings they did fly. The covering of their faces indicates deep reverence. The covering of their feet speaks of humility. Using the two remaining wings to fly denotes service. The interesting thing is that service comes last, pointing up the fact that this is not among the first things that God wants. He does not first want you to serve him, and later come to reverence and worship him. Service ought to be a product of our reverence and worship. Reverence and worship ought to precede service not only for the seraphim but for human beings like you and me.

In Revelation 4:8 there may be a possible reference to seraphim. The word translated "beast" in the King James Version ought rather to be translated "creatures." Now, since the name seraphim means "burning" in the Bible, the seraphim have been associated with purification.

In the vision of Isaiah one of the seraphim took from the altar a live coal and with it purged the lips of Isaiah. So because of this we ordinarily associate the seraphim with purification.

The second category that needs special attention are the cherubim. We find them first in the Bible as guards for the Garden of Eden. After Adam and Eve had been driven out, God stationed the cherubim at the entrance to the Garden to keep Adam and Eve from returning. They had sinned, and because of their sin they had been banished from that pellucid paradise. Had they returned they might well have eaten of the Tree of Life, which would have meant eternal physical existence. Can you imagine how horrible it would have been for this old mortal body, even after it's worn out, decayed, and diseased to continue to exist on and on and on and on? The cherubim were stationed at the Garden of Eden to keep Adam and Eve from returning and continuing their rebellion against God through the eating of still other forbidden fruit.

The cherubim are found again in Exodus 37:7–9 in connection with the mercy seat. They were in the form of beautiful golden figures, considered as protectors for the Ark of the Covenant. Some commentators have sought to make a case for the fact that the cherubim are the protectors of God's holiness. God stationed them at the Garden of Eden to protect what he said should not be touched, that was holy unto him. In the Ark of the Covenant there were objects holy to God, and in one area was the shechinah glory, which symbolized the eternal presence and holiness of God. Again, the cherubim were looked upon as protectors of that glory.

In Exodus 26:1 we find figures of the cherubim embroidered on the curtains of the tabernacle. Again, this decoration could stand for protective care for the holiness of God. This curtain upon which these images were embroidered separated between the divine presence in the holy of holies and the sinful people on the outside.

In Ezekiel we find nineteen references to the cherubim. So this is an angelic category that has special favor in the sight of God and they are generally associated with the things God would have done in this world. Let's look now at a

CLASSIFICATION

That's the classification archangel. Some commentators contend that there were several archangels. The Bible only identifies one. I believe it was the poet Milton who identified Gabriel as an archangel. But Milton is not one of the inspired writers of the sacred canon. Because of this, some think that Gabriel, along with Michael, is an archangel. However, the Bible tells us that Michael was the archangel. Arch of course means ruler, indicating the position of authority which Michael holds. He is the angel above all angels. He is most often associated with judgment. Through the ages he has been the messenger of God's vengeance, and he is looked upon as a warrior.

There's a passage in Daniel 10:21 which seems to specifically identify Michael with the nation Israel. He is referred to as Michael, your prince. In this context he could be looked upon as the Jewish angel, the one who is given specific responsibility for these people of God. Again, in Daniel 12:1, he is referred to as "the great prince which standeth for the children of thy people." Again, he is associated with the Jews. Michael appears in the twelfth chapter of the Revelation, verses 7–12, as the head of the armies to fight the victorious battle against Satan and his angels. Also, Paul, in 1 Thessalonians 4:16 wrote that at the time of the coming of Christ, when he returns to our earth, it will be with the accompaniment of the voice of the archangel. That's Michael.

Some have speculated that Lucifer was at one time an archangel. He is the fallen angel and the one that we will discuss in the chapter, "The Perverted Angel." He perverted the purpose of God, sinned and fell from his initial estate. Whatever may have been his position before his sin, he stands as the head of all demons, just as Michael stands as the head of all angels. According to the book of the Revelation, these two will meet in command of their respective armies, the forces of heaven against the forces of hell, the powers of right against the powers of wrong, and in that day there will be a final triumph for Christ and the powers of righteousness. Michael will lead the victorious armies of Christ.

Think for a moment about this other angel mentioned so prominently in the Bible. He is Gabriel. His name is said to mean, "God's hero, the mighty one, or man of God." He appears four times in the Scripture and is associated in each case with good news. He appears in Daniel 8:15 f., talking about the coming of Christ. He appears in Luke 1:19, making ready for the coming of Christ. In Luke 1:26 f. Gabriel is associated with good news. Most often when we come to talk about the Second Coming of Christ we mention Gabriel blowing his horn. Whether

Gabriel blows his horn or makes a verbal announcement matters not at all, but it is entirely possible he will be the one to announce the good news that Christ the Lord is coming, in that day when he will be crowned as King of kings and Lord of lords. Now think about their

CHORES

What are the duties that these angelic beings perform? God's holy angels have been given the responsibility of the watchcare of the church. Just as angels ministered to Jesus Christ when he was here in the flesh, so they minister today to those whom he has redeemed. They cooperate fully with and confirm the ministry of the Holy Spirit. They do not usurp the ministry of the Spirit, but they complement it in making provision for the physical needs of human beings, just as the Holy Spirit provides for the spiritual needs of human beings.

In the first place, angels give physical direction. You remember that an angel led Philip the evangelist into Samaria. There was a lost man there who needed to be saved. Philip, whose heart was on fire for Christ, was looking for an opportunity to preach. An angel pointed him in the right direction.

In Acts 10:12 an angel directed Cornelius to find the man who would relate to him the way of salvation. The angel directed Cornelius to Simon Peter, who was the man.

In the second place, angels provide physical sustenance. Angels fed Israel in the wilderness with manna. Manna is sometimes called angel's food. They provided for the people of God in an hour of grim circumstances. When

God's people were doing God's will, God provided for them through this angelic ministry. Angels provided bread for Elijah. They gave nourishment and sustenance to our Lord after his temptations, and they revealed the fact of physical safety to the apostle Paul prior to a shipwreck. An angel revealed to Paul that not a single life of the 275 people on board would be lost. Angels ministered to our Lord physically in the Garden of Gethsemane, when his body was so wracked with the anguish of the moment that perspiration came forth as drops of blood.

In John 5:4 we find physical healing coming as a result of the ministry of an angel. That's the interesting scene at the Pool of Bethesda. You might be interested to know that a portion of that balcony and pool has been excavated in recent years, and this is one of the things a person travelling through the Middle East and visiting the city of Jerusalem can see. There was a pool which, on certain occasions, had its waters troubled by an angel. At the moment the waters were troubled, the first cripple placed into the water was miraculously healed. One man said that when the water was troubled, no one was there to put him in. He had never been healed and was still a cripple, because he didn't have anyone ready at an instant's notice to push him into the water when the angel came. And so this is a case of physical healing as the result of the presence of an angel.

In the third place, angels provide physical protection. They protected Jacob from Esau. They protected Daniel from the wild lions. Little children are protected by angels, and an angel delivered Peter and the apostles in an unusual manner. They've been assigned, then, the responsibility for physical safe keeping.

In the fourth place, they encompass the church. In Hebrews 12:1 we find a passage that in all probability refers to angels: "Wherefore seeing we also are encompassed about with so great a cloud of witnesses, let us lay aside every weight, and the sin which doth so easily beset us, and let us run with patience the race that is set before us, Looking unto Jesus the author and finisher of our faith." That "so great a cloud of witnesses" could very well be the angelic hosts. It's both challenging and frightening to know that in our meetings angels are watching over us. They observe the church for protection and with satisfaction. I'm confident there is an abiding sense of joy in the being of an angel when he sees one of Christ's churches flex its muscle, stand to its full height, and begin to occupy the place that Christ has assigned it on the face of the earth. What joy there must be, not only in this cloud of witnesses that surrounds us, but all through the heavens when one sinner repents and receives Jesus Christ as Savior. The joy bells of heaven are set in motion when that happens. So it must be with deep satisfaction that angels observe the ministry of the church and rejoice in the proclamation of the gospel, in the convicting work of God's Spirit that brings the lost from darkness into light and from damnation into salvation.

A fifth chore performed by angels is that they escort the redeemed in death. Mark 13:27 tells us that at the time of the resurrection they shall gather the elect for glory and for reward. That means those who are redeemed by the blood of the Lamb and look forward to the end of time with an angelic accompaniment can say with assurance, "I won't have to cross Jordan alone."

In the sixth place, these angels will play a vital role in the second coming of Christ. Not only will they accompany Christ when he returns, but they will be assigned the responsibility "to gather out of his kingdom all things that do offend and them which do iniquity and shall cast them into a furnace of fire." They will be the instruments of vengeance, seeing to it that God's holiness and righteousness are vindicated and that those who have dared to reject the Son of God will answer for their rejection.

Today, we can choose whether or not to receive the ministry of angels. Our choice comes through our faith in Christ. If we choose Jesus Christ and follow him, we choose the protective watchcare of angels. If we reject Jesus Christ, then we choose all of the diabolical temptations of the devil and his angels. In the time of the second coming we will no longer be afforded the privilege of choice. If we delay until then, it will be everlastingly too late. That means we have the responsibility and privilege of making the most of the opportunity right now. An unsaved person chooses whether or not to have this ministry in his life, whether or not to be the recipient of God's best things.

8

THE PECULIAR ANGEL

Genesis 16:11-13

There are a number of Scriptures found in both Old and New Testaments which indicate that one angel is unique, or different, from all the rest. He is the one I have chosen to call the "peculiar angel." He is peculiar in the sense that there is not another like him. In the Old Testament he is uniformly designated "the angel of the Lord." This one word, "the," sets him apart. This is comparable to what Jesus said in John 14, verse 6, "I am *the* way, *the* truth, and *the* life," indicating there's not another way or another truth or another life. He's it! In that sense the Angel of the Lord is unique and peculiar. He's different from the others.

He not only is designated the Angel of the Lord; he also is called the Messenger of the Covenant. This title is found in Exodus 3:2 and in Malachi 3:1. In Exodus 3:2 we read, "And the angel of the Lord appeared unto him in a flame of fire out of the midst of a bush: and he looked, and, behold, the bush burned with fire, and the bush was not consumed."

There are other passages to which we can point, but let's take a look at the one in Malachi 3:1. "Behold, I will send my messenger, and he shall prepare the way before me: and the Lord, whom ye seek, shall suddenly come to his temple, even the messenger of the covenant, whom ye delight in: behold, He shall come, saith the Lord of hosts." Now let's take a moment and look at some

INDICATIONS

of this peculiar angel. The very first of the 273 references to angels in the Bible is found in Genesis 16, the passage noted under the title. Hagar, the servant of Sarai, had fled from the tent of Abraham. In chapter 16, verse 7 we read "And the angel of the Lord found her by a fountain of water in the wilderness, by the fountain in the way to Shur." In the ensuing conversation this unique angel revealed his omniscience. He not only knew the future, but he made promises to Hagar that only God could make. That is the reason why, in Genesis 16:13, we find she responded by calling him, "Thou God seest me." It is apparent this woman knew she was in the very presence of the Lord himself.

In Genesis 18, verse 1, "And the Lord appeared unto him [that is, Abraham] in the plains of Mamre: and he sat in the tent door in the heat of the day." In this very interesting experience from the life of Abraham, we find that the Angel of the Lord spoke directly and revealed to Abraham some of the things that would happen in the future. Abraham saw three men, but in verse 3 he addressed one of them as "my Lord" and said, "My Lord, if now I have found favour in thy sight, pass not away, I pray thee, from thy servant." I believe it's clear that Abraham also felt himself to be in the presence of God.

In verse 10 of chapter 18 the angel said, "I will certainly return unto thee according to the time of life; and lo, Sarah thy wife shall have a son. And Sarah heard it in the tent door, which was behind him." He predicted the future, uncovering or unveiling an experience that would occur in the life of Abraham and his wife.

Two of the angels departed, you'll recall. But the Lord, the third, remained with Abraham. They discussed together the fate of Sodom.

After this experience we find the Angel of the Lord appearing on the Mount of Sacrifice. When the hand of Abraham was stretched forth with the knife, the Angel of the Lord called unto him out of heaven and said, "Abraham, Abraham." A second time the Angel called unto him, and in verse 17 made such promises that no created angel could ever have made. He promised to bless and multiply Abraham and his seed into eternity. Surely this was the Lord himself.

Recall something Jesus said on one occasion. He stated, "Before Abraham was, I am." Then in Genesis 22, which relates the experience on the mount, in verse 18, we have a further identification. In this verse the Angel has indicated the blessing of God upon this man and upon his seed, and the blessing that they shall be to all the nations of the earth because "Thou hast obeyed My voice." We're not called upon to obey the voice of angels at any point, but we are called upon throughout the Word of God to obey the voice of God.

Another indication comes in the thirty-second chapter of Genesis. You'll want to turn to this and find, beginning in verse 24, reading through 32, the experience of Jacob who wrestled with an angel: "And Jacob was left alone;

and there wrestled a man with him until the breaking of the day. And when he saw that he prevailed not against him, he touched the hollow of his thigh; and the hollow of Jacob's thigh was out of joint, as he wrestled with him. And he said, Let me go, for the day breaketh. And he said, I will not let thee go, except thou bless me. And he said unto him, What is thy name? And he said, Jacob. And he said, Thy name shall be called no more Jacob, but Israel: for as a prince hast thou power with God and with men, and hast prevailed. And Jacob asked him, and said, Tell me, I pray thee, thy name. And he said, Wherefore is it that thou dost ask after my name? And he blessed him there. And Jacob called the name of the place Peniel: for I have seen God face to face, and my life is preserved." Jacob understood that he was in the presence of very God. "I have seen God face to face." Not just one of God's messengers, not just an angel whom God has dispatched for a purpose, but Jacob understood he was in the presence of almighty God. Hosea, in chapter 12, verses 4 and 5, bears witness to this same event. He states that it was none other than the God of hosts who wrestled with Jacob.

Again, in Exodus 3:2, Moses beheld the Angel of God in the burning bush: "And the angel of the Lord appeared unto him in a flame of fire out of the midst of a bush." Verse 2 says, "The Angel of the Lord." It continues: "And he looked and, behold, the bush burned with fire, and the bush was not consumed. And Moses said I will now turn aside, and see this great sight, why the bush is not burnt." Now get this: "And when the Lord saw that he turned aside to see, God called unto him out of the midst of the bush, and said, Moses, Moses. And he said, Here am I." I believe it's apparent that this Angel is identified as being God Himself. This Angel in the burning bush identified himself as "the God of Thy Father, the God of Abraham, the God of Isaac, and the God of Jacob" in verse 6. "And Moses hid his face; for he was afraid to look upon God." It was in that burning bush that Moses confronted the shechinah glory of almighty God, and the voice which he heard was none other than the voice of God. He hid his face, not because he was afraid to look at an angel, but because he was afraid of looking upon God. You'll recall also in this passage that the angel is identified as "I am that I am." These are some of the indications, and now, if you will, let's note some

IMPLICATIONS

based on these Scriptures. The implication, in my judgment, is clear that the Angel of the Lord in the Old Testament is none other than the pre-incarnate Christ. Contrary to the methods and the mission of the other angels, this peculiar angel, this unique angel, received the intercession or the prayer of Abraham. We're not told to pray to ordinary angels, but the Angel of the Lord received Abraham's intercession. Hagar recognized him and acknowledged him as "Thou God." In his interview with Moses he gave himself that incommunicable title, "I am that I am."

This same preexistent Angel, the gracious, loving Christ, was with Israel in the wilderness. He was their guide in the form of a pillar of cloud by day and a pillar of fire by night. He was their provider in that he sent manna when they were hungry. Every need they had was supplied. In Numbers 20:16 we find that credit is given to this Angel for the deliverance of the Jews from Egypt. "And when we cried unto the Lord, he heard our voice, and sent an angel, and hath brought us forth out of Egypt: and, behold, we are in Kadesh, a city in the uttermost of thy border." So the Angel of the Lord received credit for having brought the people out of the land of bondage. In Isaiah 63:9 it is pointed out that "the Angel of his presence saved them: in his love and in his pity he redeemed them; and he bear them, and he carried them all the days of old." In other words, the loving providence and the compassion of God revealed in Jesus Christ in the pages of the New Testament is not really new. It's simply an extension of what God was revealing to his people who had spiritual eyes with which to see all through the Old Testament. Jesus Christ is the same yesterday, today, and forever. When in love and compassion he ministered to his people, the people of Israel, he simply was revealing what we have found to be true of him in his life, his death, his burial, and his resurrection here on earth. Other Scriptures give us additional implications, but let's look at the

INCARNATION

It's interesting to note that the Jewish writers consistently interpret the phrase "the Angel of the Lord" as referring to the Messiah. The Jews only accept the Old Testament, but when they read and interpret the Scriptures their scholars construe this angel as being a foregleam of Messiah. They gave him the name Metatron. Ancient Jewish scholars called him the "Angel of Countenance," because he sees and beholds God's countenance continuously.

One statement from the Talmud declares the Metatron, the Angel of the Lord, is united with the most high God by oneness of nature. So the Jewish writers see God himself being revealed to human beings in this Metatron. Another Jewish source speaks of this angel as having dominion over all created things.

Now think for a moment about a New Testament verse. In Hebrews 1:1–2, we read: God, Who at sundry times and in divers manners spake in time past unto the fathers by the prophets, Hath in these last days spoken unto us by his Son." God chose to reveal himself in different ways in the Old Testament, and one of these ways was through the Angel of the Lord. But finally the ultimate revelation came when Jesus Christ, God's Son incarnate in human flesh, came to reveal the heart of God to the mind and life of man.

The New Testament does not make the same kind of reference to the Angel of the Lord. In fact, there are many places in the New Testament where we have a reference to "the Angel." These, however, are not the same as the Old Testament references and do not imply that angel is synonymous with Jesus Christ the Son of God. In the New Testament the Son of God appeared in human form and there is no further need for God to reveal himself in this unique way through the Angel of the Lord.

In the book of Revelation, however, as the apostle John is drawing back the curtain to show us something of the last things that will take place on this earth, we find the Lord Jesus appearing again under the symbolical name,

Angel. I believe that's what we have in this tenth chapter of Revelation. This might well be a reminder to us that the Angel of the Covenant of the Old Testament, who acts again in fulfilling the Covenant promises remembering mercy in wrath, will be the One to bring about the end of this present age, the cessation of time and the commencement of the kingdom age. I believe we do well to know Christ's part in all of this.

In the tenth of Revelation he is described as "the mighty Angel, crowned with a rainbow." Recall the significance of the rainbow. It was the sign of the covenant of God with his people in ancient times. This mighty Angel, whom I construe to be Jesus Christ the Son of God, will come in perfect fulfilment of all of God's promises to do that which God has said he would do for his people.

We find that Angel, in Revelation 10, standing upon the sea and the land, one foot on the land and one foot on the sea, and he calls to a close all the affairs of men and brings time to its end. What a marvelous picture this is of our Lord, who is ready to assert his dominion and authority over both land and sea and who has the authority to close out man's affairs. In that day, he who has all authority and all power, will be crowned King of kings and Lord of lords. In that day, "the Kingdoms of this world are become the Kingdoms of our Lord and of his Christ and he shall reign forever and forever."

If he were to appear now, how would you stand in his presence? What would your status be? According to his own word, you can either be for him or against him, but no neutrality is allowed. Maybe you've tried to ride the fence. Maybe you've tried to live an uncommitted life.

Possibly you've thought you could drift by or slide through, and that it made no difference. It'll make all the difference in the world when Christ returns, for eternity depends upon your commitment. If you're not committed to Christ, then your commitment is against him.

9

THE PERVERTED ANGEL

Isaiah 14:12-15

The Bible describes two kinds of angels, those referred to as the elect or holy angels, and the fallen angels. The fallen angels are those who sinned and who fell from their original estate. Around these fallen angels are associated all the sin and evil in our world, including unclean spirits and demons.

Jesus repeatedly referred to demons and unclean spirits. Some New Testament commentators suggest that Jesus merely accommodated himself to the religious prejudices of his time, and the country in which he grew up. They continue by saying that Jesus did not really believe in demons and unclean spirits, but that he simply assumed the beliefs of the people to whom he was ministering. The fact is, if Jesus had been the kind to accommodate himself to the beliefs and understanding of his generation, he never would have been rejected and crucified. If it had been his purpose to be "one of the boys," assuming the same stance and idealogy as those to whom he preached, he would have been accepted by other people and would never have been killed for the differences that he proclaimed.

The followers of Jesus Christ would never have knowingly exposed themselves to scorn, persecution, and death for a religion of accommodation. If their religion had been based on a chameleon type of faith, that took on the color, texture, and fiber of that with which it was associated, I cannot imagine the twelve or any of the other Christian martyrs giving their lives for that sort of faith. The followers of Christ suffered and died for what they believed to be true! They believed so strongly that they were willing to give their lives for the perpetuation of those beliefs.

Lucifer, called "the son of the morning," became Satan by his sin. His was the first sin in all creation. It came long before the sin of Adam and Eve; and, because of his sin, he who once enjoyed the estate of an angel became the adversary of God. He is found under approximately forty different titles in the pages of God's Word. He is called the adversary, he is called the accuser, roaring lion, Beelzebub, a liar and the father of all lies, and on and on.

My question to you is, "Do you believe in the devil? It is no sign of superior intelligence to disbelieve in a literal, personal devil. It is the sign of intelligent faith to accept the teachings of Jesus Christ, believing even where we cannot fully explain. Remember first the

DENIAL

of this perverted angel. The fact of Lucifer's sin is difficult for us to handle intellectually. I don't understand it, and I'm sure you would have to agree that you do not either. The sin of Adam and Eve is much more understandable, for Eve was influenced by Satan. When it comes to the sin of Lucifer this could not have been the case, for Lucifer, or Satan, in his original estate was not surrounded by any evil or temptation to sin. There was no external influence leading him to rebel against God's law. God didn't create the temptation, therefore the temptation must have come as a result of internal thought and purpose.

How did it come about? It came about because angels, just like human beings, were given God's finest, best gift. They were granted the gift of free moral choice. Angels have the privilege of choosing whether to follow God or themselves. Lucifer chose to follow himself, to exhalt his own ego.

It's generally agreed that the sin of Lucifer was pride. Now if you'll turn to 1 Timothy 3:6, you'll find a passage of Scripture that seems to indicate this. In that verse we read, "Not a novice, lest being lifted up with pride ye fall into the condemnation of the devil." Now what is the condemnation of the Devil? This probably refers to the sin of Lucifer or Satan. This alone is not conclusive, but I believe our text in Isaiah is. In these brief verses, 14:12–15, Lucifer said: I will exalt . . . I will sit . . . I will ascend . . . I will be like. . . ." When he asserted his own authority, he rejected the sovereignty of God. When he said, "I'll do it my way," he said, "I'll not do it God's way," for his way was not God's way.

Because sin cannot exist in the presence of the holiness and majesty of God, Lucifer was banished from heaven. He was kicked out. Because of the holiness and purity of God, he cannot tolerate the presence of iniquity and blackness of sin.

God's plan of salvation comes into play at this point, for no one of us can produce the holiness, righteousness, and purity God demands. How can we become acceptable to God? How can we reach the point where God will allow us to dwell in his presence eternally in heaven? The only way possible is for Jesus Christ, in his perfection, to cover our imperfections through the blood. Then God sees us not as sinful wretches, not as rebellious derelicts, but he sees us in the perfection of Jesus Christ. Friend, that's what it's all about! That's the way one is saved.

Lucifer, because of his sin, could not continue to exist in the presence of a morally perfect God. God did not make Lucifer sin, God made Lucifer and Lucifer made sin by his own choice. Now see some of the

DETAILS

surrounding this. Turn to 2 Peter 2:4, and you'll find there a reference to "the angels that sinned." Because of the exhalted position which Lucifer originally held, because he apparently was superior to other angels, he was able successfully to use his influence in bringing other angels into sin and banishment from heaven. These angels that sinned are identified in the words of our Lord, when he referred to "the devil and his angels" to include not only Lucifer but the others who sinned. These angels do not belong to Lucifer, or Satan, by an act of creation, but they belong to Lucifer in spirit, for theirs is a spirit of rebellion against the sovereignty of God. They're associated with him in that regard. Just as Michael has a position of ascendency over other angels, for Michael is called "the archangel," so Lucifer had a position that was exhalted among angels. Therefore in his sin he became the leader of the forces of opposition.

Having been banished from heaven in disgrace, Satan has a plan and program for opposing God. I hope you understand this. I think anyone can grasp it. Lucifer hates God. He also hates all of those who belong to God, and he still wants to control the universe and overthrow all of God's influence. Taking a devious route, Satan, or Lucifer, carries out his warfare against God by attacking man. This is his plan. He cannot attack God directly. He does not have that power. His power is limited. It all began with the temptation of Adam and Eve, and it has continued in this very moment until your life and mine.

I am reminded of a little morsel, in which a friend said that unless he hits the devil in a headon collision every morning, he becomes fearful that he and the devil are going in the same direction! Satan has continued to carry out his plan and purpose through all of the millenia of the existence of humanity. Against God's highest creation, mankind, Satan and his angels direct their frontal attack.

Evidence of his work is everywhere. Where I see disease and suffering and temptation and sin and poverty and ignorance and iniquity and death, I'm reminded of the fact that the perfect and holy God who created this earth is not the author of confusion and sin. Confusion and sin are a result of the devil's work, for he constantly continues to interfere with God's plan by attacking human beings.

Many years ago a camel driver was taking a caravan across the desert. One morning he said to his people, "We had visitors in the area last night." They looked at him in surprise and asked how he knew. They had neither heard nor seen anyone. His proof was he had discovered the tracks of the intruders in the sand. If you do not believe in the devil, open your eyes and look at his tracks. Go into the hospitals, the ghettos, the asylums, and the holes of our society, and you'll find his presence and power proven conclusively. That's the way the devil operates. He is still using the same plan to tear down, wreck, and destroy God's highest creation, mankind. Remember what the Bible teaches about Satan's

DEFEAT

Lucifer's days are numbered. If you follow him, your days are also numbered. As wretched and miserable as Satan and his angels are now, there will be an infinite increase in their torment after God pronounces sentence upon them in judgment. Open your Bibles again to Matthew 8. In verses 28 and 29 Jesus had a direct confrontation with two of Satan's angels.

Now remember the name "angel" does not imply goodness. The name "angel" means messenger. An angel may be a holy angel or a fallen angel, but most of us have associated the word angel with the elect angels or the holy angels. Satan also has his angels, and they are his messengers.

In this passage Jesus confronted two of Satan's angels. These demons knew who Jesus was and asked this question: "Art thou come hither to torment us *before the time?*" There we find an open recognition on their part of their future condition. They know they're on the losing team. They know that there's no way to win the ultimate victory against the power of God as it is revealed through Jesus Christ. It's because of this consciousness of the inevitable on the part of the demons that they have redoubled their efforts in an attempt to drag down and destroy God's highest creation.

The Bible teaches that in the last days things will grow unbelievably worse. The world's wickedness will be more and more open. There'll be more lewdness, more sexual perversion, more obscenity, more nudity, pornography, and unspeakable evils sweep across our nation than ever before. The Bible teaches that unrestrained sin will sweep our world like a tidal wave before the coming of Jesus Christ. Why? Because the devil and all of his angels know that their days are numbered, and whatever digs they intend to get in, they have to get them in quickly.

Thank God, Christians don't have to be overcome by tidal waves of lawlessness and iniquity. For those who are in Christ, there is an anchor that holds in every storm that comes. He who is for us is greater than he who is against us. It's still gloriously true that "the blood of Jesus Christ, God's Son, cleanseth us from all sin." It is likewise true that our blessed Lord who loves us with an everlasting love will never leave us nor forsake us.

When the going gets rough, when the battle is at its height in fury, we don't have to look around for our ally, for he's standing right with us and promised never to leave us. He not only has promised his presence, but he has also placed at our disposal all the resources of heaven with which to fight and win against Satan. The same power in which Jesus Christ repelled the devil and won the ultimate victory is made available to you and me in direct measure to our needs. Whatever our temptations, whatever our tendency to sin, whatever debilitating habit may have its grip upon us, the power of heaven is available and we can win the victory through Jesus Christ.

We have available the sword of the Spirit, the breastplate of righteousness, the shield of faith; our loins are girt about with truth; our feet are shod with the preparation of the Gospel of peace; and we wear the helmet of God's salvation. Satan, the father of all lies, will try to keep you on his side, but friend, don't be defeated! You can get on the winning side when you give your life in faith to Jesus Christ. That's the glorious message of God. You don't have to join the ranks of the perverted angels, you don't have to be a pervert in the sight of God, you can be one of God's own soldiers and stand tall and straight in the battle taking place. And when the final trumpet sounds, you'll be numbered in that victorious army that has overcome the world.